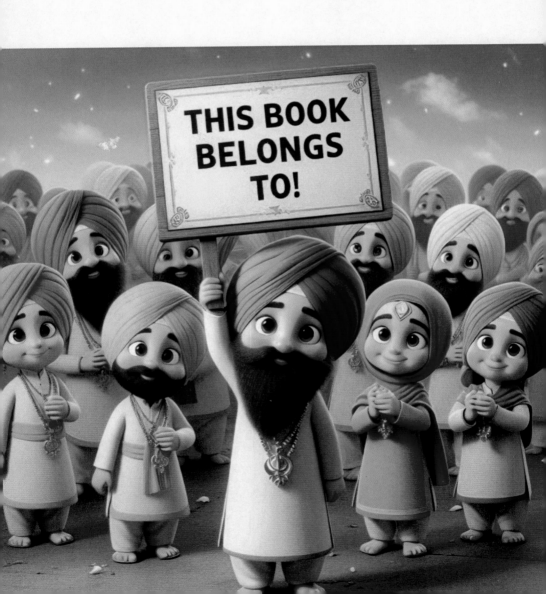

SAT SRI AKAAL!

I, AM DELIGHTED TO WELCOME YOU TO A MAGICAL JOURNEY THROUGH THE ENCHANTING WORLD OF
"IK ONKAR: ONE BIG MAGICAL MESSAGE FOR KIDS."
THIS STORY BEGINS WITH A BRIGHT AND CURIOUS GIRL NAMED KYNA KAUR, WHO, JUST LIKE YOU, HAD A HEART FULL OF QUESTIONS.

KYNA, WITH HER INNOCENT EYES AND A SPIRIT OF WONDER, APPROACHED HER WISE GRANDMOTHER TO UNRAVEL THE MYSTERY OF THE MOOL MANTRA. WHAT ENSUED WAS A BEAUTIFUL CONVERSATION, FULL OF WARMTH AND LOVE, ECHOING THE VERY ESSENCE OF GURU NANAK'S TEACHINGS.

IN THIS BOOK, YOU'LL DISCOVER THE SECRETS HIDDEN WITHIN THE MOOL MANTRA – A POWERFUL MESSAGE THAT HOLDS THE KEY TO LOVE, UNITY, AND UNDERSTANDING. IT'S A TREASURE, WHISPERED THROUGH GENERATIONS, WAITING TO BE EMBRACED BY YOUNG HEARTS LIKE YOURS.

TOGETHER, WE'LL EMBARK ON A JOURNEY OF LEARNING, EXPLORING THE MEANING, PRONUNCIATION, AND THE INCREDIBLE BEAUTY OF THE MOOL MANTRA IN BOTH PUNJABI AND ENGLISH. THE PAGES COME ALIVE WITH VIBRANT ILLUSTRATIONS, CREATED JUST FOR YOU, TO INSPIRE AND IGNITE YOUR IMAGINATION.

LET THE MOOL MANTRA FILL YOUR HEARTS WITH JOY AND CURIOSITY. THIS BOOK IS YOUR GUIDE, FRIEND, AND INSPIRATION TO UNRAVEL GURU NANAK'S SECRET MESSAGE.

ONE SUNNY DAY, AFTER A VISIT TO THE GURDWARA WITH GRANDMA, LITTLE KYNA COULDN'T STOP HUMMING A DELIGHTFUL TUNE. SHE SKIPPED AROUND THE HOUSE, HER HEART SINGING WITH JOY. INTRIGUED BY THE MELODY, SHE DECIDED TO SHARE IT WITH GRANDMA.

"HEY GRANDMA, LISTEN TO THIS TUNE! LALALALA!" KYNA SANG, HER EYES SPARKLING.

GRANDMA CHUCKLED, "OH, MY LITTLE SONGBIRD! THAT'S THE IK ONKAR TUNE. WOULD YOU LIKE TO KNOW MORE ABOUT IT?"

KYNA NODDED EAGERLY, "YES, YES! WHAT'S THE IK ONKAR TUNE, GRANDMA?"

GRANDMA EXPLAINED, "IT'S PART OF SOMETHING MAGICAL CALLED THE MOOL MANTRA. GURU NANAK DEV JI, A WISE AND LOVING TEACHER, WROTE IT. WE SING THE MOOL MANTRA TO CONNECT WITH THE UNIVERSE AND SPREAD LOVE."

KYNA'S EYES WIDENED WITH CURIOSITY, "WHAT'S AN IK ONKAR, GRANDMA?"

"WELL, SWEETHEART, THE MOOL MANTRA IS LIKE A COSMIC GUIDE. IT STARTS WITH 'IK ONKAR,' REMINDING US OF ONE UNIVERSAL CREATOR. IT TEACHES US TO LIVE IN TRUTH, KINDNESS, AND WONDER, JUST LIKE YOU SPREAD JOY WITH YOUR TUNES!" GRANDMA SHARED, A TWINKLE IN HER EYE.

KYNA GRINNED, "THAT'S SO COOL, GRANDMA! WHY DO WE SING IT?"

"WE SING IT TO FEEL CONNECTED TO THE UNIVERSE AND TO REMIND OURSELVES OF GURU NANAK DEV JI'S TEACHINGS. IT'S LIKE A MUSICAL LESSON IN LOVE, TRUTH, AND WONDER," GRANDMA REPLIED WITH A WARM SMILE.

EXCITED, KYNA ASKED, "CAN YOU TEACH ME MORE, GRANDMA?"

SO, GRANDMA SHARED THE MOOL MANTRA WITH KYNA, WORD BY WORD. KYNA LISTENED CAREFULLY, ABSORBING THE MAGICAL WORDS THAT HELD THE KEY TO A HAPPY AND MEANINGFUL LIFE.

AS DAYS WENT BY, KYNA DECIDED TO SHARE THE LESSONS OF THE MOOL MANTRA WITH HER FRIENDS AND FAMILY. SHE TOLD THEM ABOUT BEING TRUTHFUL, KIND, AND FINDING WONDER IN EVERYDAY THINGS.

KYNA'S FRIENDS JOINED IN, CREATING A CIRCLE OF JOY AND LOVE. THEY EMBRACED THE MOOL MANTRA TEACHINGS, JUST LIKE LITTLE KYNA. AND AFTER THE STORY ENDS, THERE'S A LITTLE NOTE THAT ENCOURAGES ALL THE KIDS READING TO EXPLORE THE MOOL MANTRA, LEARN GURU NANAK DEV JI'S SECRET MESSAGE, AND SPREAD LOVE AND KINDNESS IN THEIR OWN MAGICAL WAY.

KYNA, INSPIRED BY THE MOOL MANTRA, KEPT THE
ENCHANTING MELODY PLAYING IN THE BACKGROUND IN HER
ROOM. IT HELPED HER SLEEP PEACEFULLY, KNOWING THAT
WAHEGURU WAS ALWAYS THERE, WATCHING OVER HER. IN
THAT CALM STATE, SURROUNDED BY THE SOOTHING NOTES,
LITTLE KYNA DREAMT SWEET DREAMS FILLED WITH LOVE AND
WONDER.

AND SO, THE VILLAGE ECHOED WITH THE HAPPY TUNES OF THE
MOOL MANTRA, AS LITTLE KYNA AND HER FRIENDS DANCED
THROUGH LIFE, SPREADING LOVE AND LAUGHTER WHEREVER
THEY WENT.

"LET THE MOOL MANTAR BE YOUR GUIDING STAR, LIGHTING UP YOUR HEART WITH LOVE, COURAGE, AND THE MAGIC OF ONENESS.

IN ITS WORDS, DISCOVER A UNIVERSE OF WISDOM WAITING TO UNFOLD, JUST FOR YOU."

THERE IS ONLY ONE GOD

ਸਤਿ ਨਾਮੁ

WHOSE NAME IS TRUTH

ਕਰਤਾ ਪੁਰਖੁ

HE IS THE CREATOR

KARTA PURKH:

HE IS THE CREATOR OF EVERYTHING.

GOD MADE THE WHOLE WORLD, THE MOUNTAINS, AND THE OCEANS!

HE'S SUPER CREATIVE!

NIRBHAU

ਨਿਰਭਉ

HAS NO FEAR

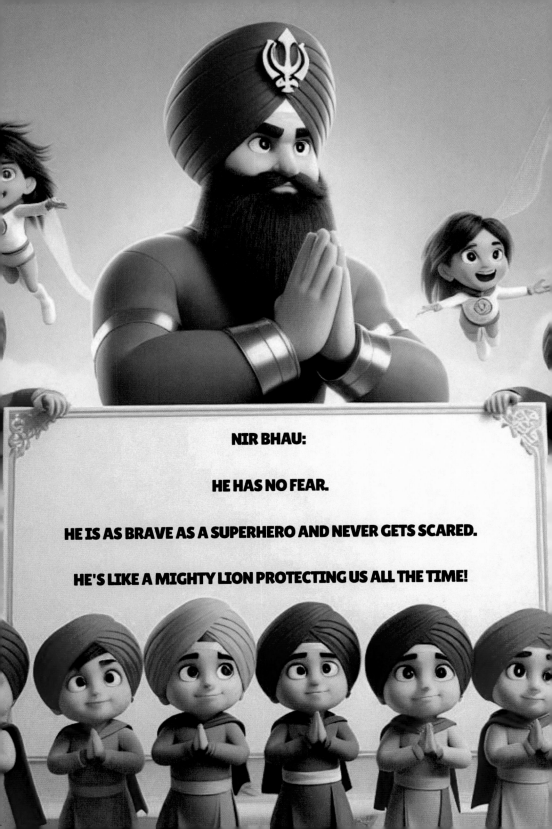

NIR BHAU:

HE HAS NO FEAR.

HE IS AS BRAVE AS A SUPERHERO AND NEVER GETS SCARED.

HE'S LIKE A MIGHTY LION PROTECTING US ALL THE TIME!

ਨਿਰਵੈਰੁ

HAS NO HATE

NIR VAIR:

HE HAS NO HATE.

HE LOVES EVERYONE, JUST LIKE HOW YOU LOVE YOUR FAMILY AND FRIENDS.

HE'S LIKE A BIG HUG FROM THE SKY!

AKAAL MOORAT

ਅਕਾਲ ਮੂਰਤਿ

HE IS BEYOND TIME

AKAAL MOORAT:

HE LIVES FOREVER AND DOESN'T HAVE A PHYSICAL FORM.

HE'S LIKE A MAGICAL SPIRIT WHO'S ALWAYS AROUND US.

HE'S EVERYWHERE, EVEN IF WE CAN'T SEE HIM!

ਅਜੂਨੀ ਸੈਭੰ

HE IS BEYOND BIRTH AND DEATH

AJOONI SAIBHANG:

**HE IS BEYOND BIRTH AND DEATH, NOT LIKE
US WHO ARE BORN AND GROW OLD.**

**HE'S ALWAYS BEEN HERE AND ALWAYS WILL
BE, LIKE A FOREVER FRIEND, SHINING BY
HIMSELF,**

GUR PARSAD

ਗੁਰਪ੍ਰਸਾਦਿ
WITH GURU JI'S GRACE

GUR PARSAAD:

WE CAN UNDERSTAND HIM THROUGH THE KINDNESS OF THE TRUE GURU.

JUST LIKE HOW A TEACHER HELPS YOU LEARN NEW THINGS, WISE TEACHERS HELP US UNDERSTAND MORE ABOUT GOD.

THEY'RE LIKE SPECIAL GUIDES!

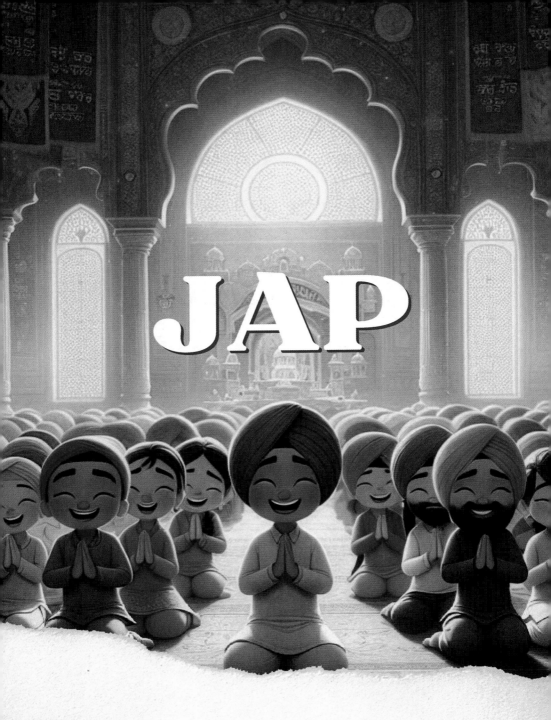

JAP

ਜਪੁ

MEDITATE ON HIS NAME

JAP:

RECITE (PRAY).

IT'S LIKE TALKING TO GOD, TELLING HIM ABOUT YOUR DAY OR ASKING FOR HELP WHEN YOU NEED IT.

IT'S LIKE HAVING A CHAT WITH YOUR BEST FRIEND!

ਆਦਿ ਸਚੁ

TRUE SINCE BEGINNING OF TIME

ਜੁਗਾਦਿ ਸਚੁ

HAS BEEN TRUE FOR AGES

JUGAAD SACH:

TRUE THROUGH AGES.

HE'S BEEN TRUE FOR A LONG, LONG TIME AND WILL ALWAYS BE.

HE'S LIKE A TIMELESS STORY THAT NEVER ENDS!

HAI BHEE SACH:

IS TRUE NOW.

EVEN TODAY, GOD'S TRUTH NEVER CHANGES.

HE'S LIKE A MOUNTAIN YOU CAN ALWAYS COUNT ON!

ਨਾਨਕ ਹੋਸੀ

GURU NANAK SAYS

NANAK HOSEE:

SAYS NANAK, WILL FOREVER BE TRUE. NANAK, A WISE PERSON, BELIEVES THAT GOD'S TRUTH WILL NEVER, EVER CHANGE, JUST LIKE THE SKY IS ALWAYS BLUE!

NANAK KNOWS THAT GOD IS FOREVER AND ALWAYS THERE FOR US, LIKE A CONSTANT FRIEND IN OUR HEARTS!

ਭੀ ਸਚੁ

WILL FOREVER BE TRUE

"BHI SACH"

MEANS "IS ALSO TRUE." IT'S LIKE ADDING ANOTHER PIECE OF TRUTH TO WHAT'S BEING DISCUSSED.

SO, WHEN YOU HEAR "BHEE SACH," IT'S LIKE SAYING, "THAT'S TRUE TOO!"

IT'S A COOL WAY OF AGREEING WITH SOMETHING OR ACKNOWLEDGING ANOTHER TRUTH IN THE CONVERSATION.

Dear Readers,

A heartfelt thank you for joining the magical journey of "Ik Onkar: One Big Magical Message for Kids"! I'm MS Chadha, the author, and I'm thrilled to share this special book inspired by my incredible daughter, Kyna.

I dedicate this book to my little sunshine, Kyna, who, at the age of 6, has embarked on her reading adventures with a heart full of love for the Mool Mantra. For the past three years, she has filled her room with the sweet melody of its message, creating an environment of positivity and learning.

Kyna's wish is to spread the joy of the Mool Mantra with other young hearts, inspiring them to embrace the beautiful teachings of Guru Nanak. This book is a reflection of her love and the desire to share the warmth and wisdom she has found in these words.

To our young readers, thank you for being a part of this journey. Your curiosity, laughter, and open hearts make every word in this book come alive. I hope "Ik Onkar" brings joy and enlightenment to your days.

As you close this book, I invite you to explore other delightful adventures in the "Sikhi for Young Hearts" series. Each story is crafted with love, designed to spark curiosity, and celebrate the spirit of Sikh teachings.

And to all our little readers, remember – the magic of learning is everlasting. Keep reading, keep exploring, and keep spreading love and kindness.

Waheguru Ji Ka Khalsa, Waheguru Ji Ki Fateh.
Warmly, MS Chadha